The
Journey
Of
Success

Against All Odds

By Pollo Prosper

The Journey Of Success *Against All Odds*

Copyright © 2017

By Pollo Prosper

Published in the United States by Birds Eye View Publishing

ISBN: 978-0-9982894-2-7

Printed in the United States of America

Dedication

I want to dedicate this book to the woman of my dreams, my beautiful wife, Laurie Prosper. Thank you, sweetheart. Thank you for believing in me and supporting me through the discovery process of my dreams.

A special thank you to Julia Jean-Baptiste for helping to make this project possible.

Table of Contents

Preface

Welcome my friend - thank you for joining me as I unfold my twenty-year story of being homeless as an immigrant to a successful American - against all odds. As you read, my hope is that this book will provide you with an in-depth and practical guide to help you live and intentional life.

Over the years, I have compiled and applied the principles on a daily basis that I will be sharing with you. They have allowed me to overcome the many obstacles throughout my journey. Trust me, it has been a journey filled with fear which have been used to break the back of impossibilities.

This book is the result of countless hours of fighting against my willpower and determination to live intentionally while discovering and pursuing my dreams. May this book be a turning point in your life where you will discover your dream(s).

– Pollo Prosper

Introduction

It doesn't matter where you are in life, how old you are, or what your goals are, more than likely you want to be successful and happy in what you are doing. The key to being successful is more than just about the money - it is about:

- Making your mark

- Identifying your passions

- Living with purpose

- Enjoying the present moment

You can achieve both internal and external success, however, before you achieve success, you have to define what success means to you. It may take a little time to pinpoint your passions, values, and interests that will give your life purpose and meaning. For example, how you would like to be remembered? What would you like your legacy to be? What are you interested in? How do you want to make the place you live a better place?

Pay attention to your actions and ask if where you are right at this moment are going to lead you to where you want to be in life.

If you find yourself daydreaming about your future or feeling bored, then you are probably disconnected from what you are doing. Spend your free time doing what you enjoy doing, rather than wasting time watching television. Cherish that free time you have to pursue your goals. This book will help you create a strategic plan for your life.

Planning is not enough. You need the education, credibility, and skills to achieve your potential. However, not all education has to be formal. Long-term training programs, certifications, and apprenticeships can work well for increasing your income and supporting you in reaching your long-term goals. This book will help you get organized, set reminders and stay motivated.

Throughout this book, I reference the importance of having God in your life. He wants you to enjoy your life and use the gifts He has given you. If you are constantly dwelling on the past or daydreaming about the future, you are missing out on living in the present moment. The past and the future are illusions, and real life takes place here and now. You will learn to silence the negative thoughts and enjoy the present moment. If negative thoughts come into your head, acknowledge them, determine it is negative, and let it fade away. Give it to God.

Some people have the tendency to compare their low points with the high points of other people's lives. You must remember that while some people's lives may seem perfect, we deal with insecurities, tragedies and difficulties. No one is immune. Instead, count your blessings and spend time each day appreciating what you do have. Think beyond material possessions and appreciate those who love you, including God.

It is my hope that this book will help you focus on what you want to do, and figure out the steps required to get you where you want to be. Do what you have to do to learn the skills needed for that position or job that you want in life. God wants you to be the best you can be, and so do I. Anything is possible.

Chapter 1:
Determination Is The Factor
For Dreams To Come True

My story begins in a village, on the wealthy and beautiful island of Haiti. For the first eight years of my life, I remember being surrounded by the most important people in my life, my grandmother, mother and three siblings. Growing up on the island had many challenges. Yet, it was not until the age of eight when I was able to take my first trip into the city, did I return to my village, with an awakening about being poor.

Before that experience, all I knew was that my mother had done a great job, as a single mother, providing the necessities for her family. My mom was always a hard worker, and that intensified after my father left. I was only three-years-old when my dad packed his bag to relocate to the United States. However, I was old enough to see that it caused great pain for my family.

Growing up, I was not exposed to religion, but somewhere along the way, I learned about God. The first thing I learned is that you don't play with Him and the second is that He is always listening. After discovering that I was poor, I remember saying something like this, "God, if you take me out of this environment, I will serve you." Sure enough, He quickly kept his side of the deal, but for me, on the other hand, it took more time.

When I was fifteen-years-old, my brother, two sisters, and I boarded our very first airplane. It was a plane that would take us to the Promised Land, or so I thought, at the time. Our trip to the United States was a bittersweet one. On the one hand, God was fulfilling His promise, but on the other hand, I was leaving the only place I knew - my home, a place of safety due to the care of my mother and grandmother.

We landed at Fort Lauderdale International Airport, and my dad, who had not seen me since the age of three, was there to pick us up. I was overcome with feelings of joy and excitement. However, the feeling was short-lived. When we arrived at my dad's domicile, a woman who said she was my stepmother greeted us. Without knowing anything about this woman, I was overcome with hatred. Immediately, I became resentful against my dad. How could it be that my mother had been working so hard to take care of us while he was living the good life with this woman? My resentment came out in my actions and words. Before things got better between my father and I, they quickly grew worse. It became so bad that on a cool evening in November of 1995, my life took another life-changing turn.

On that November night, my dad and I got into a huge fight over my stepmother. In rage and anger, I ended up breaking many items in the house. As a result of this incident, my dad said these words to me," Get out now." He told his youngest son that he would no longer be responsible for him. Yes, my dad had now officially chosen his girlfriend over me and that made me homeless. With my clothes outside the house and with no place to go, I found myself pacing back and forth in the parking lot.

At this point, the reality of what had just happened hit me like a ton of bricks. For the first time in my life, I cried and sobbed. I was confused, but knew at that moment that the decisions I made would be ones of survival. I took a deep breath and became a man.

Just a few months after landing in the United States, I hooked up with a guy by the name of Charles (also known as Zoe). Charles was also from Haiti and came to the United States in the hopes of having a better future. Although we were from the same island, we only connected while we were in Fort Lauderdale. Over the years, he turned out to be a good friend and whom I credit for being alive today. After being thrown out the house, I told Charles what had happened. He was in total shock to the point where he became speechless before asking me what I was going to do. Then, I became speechless.

Over the course of a year and a half, I was partially able to stay with my cousin in their small apartment. Although I was grateful for a place to lay my head, the living conditions were not right. My three older cousins and I shared one of the two bedrooms. During this time, I was determined to do what had to be done to change the course of my life.

Keep in mind that throughout this entire ordeal, I was a young man from Haiti who grew up speaking only Creole and was unfamiliar with the English language. During this whole time, Charles and I were determined to learn and master English. Until that time came, Charles and I created our own English words. We called it 'sling-gish' because it was a combination of street English and broken English.

Miami Ghetto

It was embarrassing when we would speak to people with our new language but we were willing to endure the laughter and embarrassment for a little while. Our desire to learn the language was stronger than our fears of criticism. Charles and I understood that English would connect us to money and I could not afford to be miscommunicated.

At this point, I was broke and homeless. There is a difference, in life, between being broke and not having money. When you don't have money, your options are limited, but when you are broke, you absolutely have no options, so we were determined to learn the language for our survival and that determination paid off. In ninety days, Charles and I were both speaking English fluently.

In learning the Universal language, I was in a better position to seek jobs that would allow me to move toward greater freedom. My first job, after being kicked out of the house, was at a restaurant. I started working for $4.25 an hour to clean tables. A few days into my position, the dishwasher guy did not show up, and so I was asked by the supervisor to fill in for him. I quickly accepted the challenge. What challenge might you ask? Well, it was the problem of using a machine that I had never even heard of before and being asked to use one.

After a sixty-second training, I was able to complete that shift with a feeling that I was born to wash dishes. Many things happen in our lives, and they don't just happen by chance. My new position, and my twenty-five cent raise, placed me in a position, not only to earn more money, but also to gain work experience that could help me later in life. As faith would have it, I did not have to wait long to utilize the lessons from my first job.

Again, I found myself at another turning point; however, I was a little bit clearer about what I needed to do and how to get there. One of the greatest challenges you can face in your life is the problem of not knowing how to do something and choose to start it anyway, until you figure out how to do it. Take caution in the process. In my life, the process caused me to suffer physical, emotional and spiritual abuse. There were many days when I couldn't afford to buy food to eat. The stupidity of my pride caused me to go without food because I didn't want to ask for help. However, I thank God for real friends who know what you need even in those times when you may not be clear about what you need.

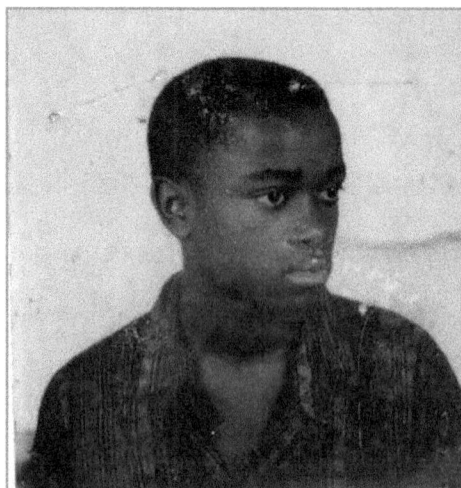

A few months after I had been promoted to dishwasher at the restaurant, an opportunity to work at another restaurant became available. After applying, as a favor to a friend, the supervisor quickly hired me at the rate of $7.75 an hour. In less than a year, my pay had almost doubled. However, I was still homeless and hungry. My supervisor, who could never pronounce my name, was a very nice guy and somehow found out about my less than ideal social situation. In an act of kindness, he allowed me to eat the customer's returned meals and leftovers. For this reason, I found myself going to work before my shift started so I could have a hot meal.

Throughout this entire period, I was able to manage school and work. It was a challenge, so much so, that I found myself making the decision to drop out of school toward the end of my last year of high school. It would be a year and a half until I no longer had to take advantage of my supervisor's generosity.

In an environment where I knew was already behind, I made it my goal to work harder than most. My drive to succeed was a combination of self-gratification and a passion for proving my stepmother wrong. She would live to see the day her words would fall to the ground and die. According to my father's girlfriend, who I nicknamed 'wicked stepmother,' she said, "He is going to end up selling drugs or die in prison."

These words played over and over in my head and I became more and more determined to press towards the mark. While others were working on looking for an opportunity, I knew that I was going to create my own opportunity. I knew that I could not allow myself to be caught up with the idea of doing 'just enough' to get a paycheck and keep my job; instead, I kept my mind on doing more than expected so that I would make something more of myself. Although I didn't realize it, I was becoming intentional about creating a personal growth plan. In the years to come, I became more and more intentional about where I was going and how I would get there.

Around 2004, I began working for the largest retail company in the world -Wal-Mart. It was growing fast. In one year, the company opened about three hundred other retail stores around the world. As the company grew, I made up my mind that I was going to grow with them. However, as I looked around at co-workers with their postsecondary degrees and years of experience in the industry, I immediately knew I needed to rethink my old strategy. Yes, it had gotten me to this point, but the question became, would it take me to the next level? In pondering on that question, I knew the answer was no.

I would need a new strategy and had to implement it fast. I created a plan that could work and decided to work harder, stay at work longer, and volunteer for more projects. As I implemented this plan, I realized that it was working, but not at the pace I needed to achieve my goal. I started tweaking my plan and found myself asking this question, "How can I stand out from the crowd?" Then it hit me like a ton of bricks; it was a feeling similar to the day my father kicked me out of the house. This time, I was headed down a path with greater clarity.

In this clarity, I realized that to stand out from amongst my peers, I would have to become intentional and driven by leadership development. In my pursuit of personal leadership development, I became very familiar with the self-help section of Amazon. I started dissecting every development book I could get my hands on. I was hungry for more, and as my local church began offering leadership courses, I attended, not one, but every session. People started to notice, and in less than a year of beginning my personal growth journey, while at the company, I received my first of many promotions.

I saw results. After six months with my first promotion as department lead, I was now the lead over five departments. I remained at this level for two years until I became the second in charge of the store in South Florida. Despite my success, I was driven to learn, grow, and find out more. I became a growth junky.

It has been almost twenty years since my journey began and I would never think about trading the lessons that I have learned. As a now Certified International Coach, Trainer, and Speaker, I can honestly say that my life is a story of "Success Against the Odds." My goal and passion in life are to help others to live their best life. I want to see people reach their full potential, in life. In my pursuit to make this a reality, I needed to become a part of an organization or team where their foundation was built on the principles of adding value to others. During my research, I discovered that the John Maxwell Team was a great fit to help me reach my goals. As a result, I joined the John Maxwell Team to become a Certified Speaker, Coach, and Trainer.

The John Maxwell Team Leadership content has helped me to discover how to have a structured and practical plan in place to avoid becoming overwhelmed and less stressed. I have personally applied these techniques to enhance my own productivity, development and decision making skills to have more of a balanced lifestyle. Over the last six years, I have been studying and implementing the philosophies behind personal development, the role of influence and the effects of vision and emotions in leadership. My life is definitely a story of "Success Against the Odds."

Chapter 2:
Even In the Dictionary, Struggle Precedes Success

Are you willing to pay the price to prosper? Successes are personal but never private and include sacrifices that must be made to achieve them. Most people I've met are unwilling to ask themselves three of the most important questions related to personal success and the development of one's dream. Here are those issues that somehow go unanswered:

1. Do I have a dream?

2. Have I taken responsibility for my dream?

3. Am I willing to pay the price for success, even to the point of failure, to fulfill my dream?

Many times, we cross paths with people who have a desire to be successful, but in many instances, they are unwilling to do what it takes to achieve it. As a result of this mental stagnation, you find many individuals who stand still and do nothing because they were unable to connect with the idea of failure.

In life, many people fail to see that within their present failure lays the key to their next open door. As the cliché goes,

"When one door closes another one opens."

Recently, I read an article that was published by

https://www.uky.edu/~eushe2/Pajares/OnFailingG.html . Throughout this article, I came across

some examples of some of the greatest men in history, who overcame failure and adversity.

Their ability to overcome failure occurred when they realized that it was their responsibility to

give birth to their dream and because of their tenacious spirit, many of us now reap the rewards

from their unwillingness to stop at failure.

Did you know that Abraham Lincoln, the sixteenth president of the United States, failed

at his first attempt as a businessman? In his first attempt to be nominated for Congress, he was

defeated and his application to be commissioner of the General Land-office was rejected. Former

President, Abraham Lincoln, lost the senatorial election of 1854, the vice-presidency in 1856,

and his senatorial election of 1858. Despite his failures *and* as a result of his failures, we all

know that this great man became known for issuing the Emancipation Proclamation.

Did you know that Sir Winston Churchill, the former Prime Minister of the United

Kingdom, repeated a grade during elementary school and was placed in the lowest division in the class? Twice, he failed the entrance exam to the Royal Military Academy at Sandhurst. In his

first attempt to serve in Parliament, Sir Churchill was unable to claim a seat. He did, however,

become Prime Minister at the age of sixty-two. He first served in that position from 1940-1945

and then again from 1951-1955. In the later years of his life, he wrote one of the most recited

quote "Never give in, never give in, never, never, never, never-in nothing, great or small, large or

petty never give in except to convictions of honor and good sense, Never, Never, Never, Never

give up."

Did you know that one of his teachers described physicist Albert Einstein as being

"mentally slow," because of his delay in speaking and reading? Albert Einstein began to read,

and not until the age of seven, did he start to learn how to read. Despite these beginning

adversities, Albert Einstein was a well-renowned physicist, and he received, in 1921, the Nobel

Peace Prize in Physics for his work toward the evolution of the quantum theory.

After taking a closer look at the obstacles and barriers that faced these three men, it is

nothing short of amazing that they were each able to rise above their setbacks to become men of

great notoriety and stature in society. Abraham Lincoln, Winston Churchill and Albert Einstein

were men who played significant roles in changing the modern world. We are unable to deny their contributions in history, and their decision to continue, even when failure loomed, is nothing short of courageous. As they continued pressing through even in failure, their success was lurking at the other end. I love this quote by British Prime Minister Winston Churchill. "Success is going from failure to failure without losing enthusiasm."

You may recall earlier in my story where I stated that I became a man. It was around that same time that I realized I was responsible for everything that happened to me after that. I also decided that it was my responsibility to be the driving force towards my own success. I would have to take the steps and carry out the necessary actions to become successful. In the earlier part of my life, I believed that success would be easy to attain. I was so wrong. Let's just say I was young and stupid.

As I gained a greater understanding about the road to success, it became very hard for me to take on the responsibility for my success. Could it be that I was not prepared? Could it be that I didn't understand the actual cost of success? In the years following my decision to be a man and to be responsible for my own success, I quickly realized that success had an even greater price that needed to be paid than what I had given in the past. In analyzing the life of men like Abraham Lincoln and Winston Churchill, I would begin to realize that not one of them had achieved success without paying a high price.

I had to learn how to visualize my own success.

What does success look like?

As I began to identify my dreams and focus in on them, I began the process of internalizing the results of my thoughts about my future. I had made up my mind that I was not about to become one of those people who worked harder at their job than they did on their dream. Somehow, I was convinced, or had convinced myself, that I didn't have to align myself with a group that often became stuck in the "What if?" mode of life. What if I had pursued my dream?

For many people, the "What if?" mode intensifies because they believe that they would have to leave their nine to five job to work their dream. And although this statement holds true for many, it does not hold true for all. In my own life, I have proven that a person can have a job and still pursue their dream, especially when they don't realize that the two are taking place simultaneously. Wow, that nugget just dropped right there, it was the beginning of a new discovery for me.

Ok, I get it. There are a few of you who didn't have to go the latter route. You had an opportunity to map out your dream and even be intentional about living your dream. I would love to say that I was presented with that opportunity; however, I was not. I had to make a conscious decision to work my dream as I pursued a career, at my job.

I had to look at every day as a new opportunity to keep my dream in front of me and with focus. It became the catalyst for strengthening my deepest thoughts and preparing me for the next chapter of my life. I had to learn how to keep my eyes on the prize for what I wanted, so that I wouldn't occupy the void.

I can remember once, while seated in church, I heard the preacher say, "A man who does not know what he wants out of life, will not know the way to live his life."

When you chose to buy this book, I would like to recognize and acknowledge you as my friend. Friends are people who share with each other, so from one friend to another, I want to let you in on a little secret. If you don't know what you want out of life, you will not know the way to live your life. Do you know that you possess the same ability as the most successful person in the universe? The reason they are successful is not what they are doing, rather, it is the way that they are doing it. Which causes them to stand out from the pack?

One of the greatest things I admire about successful individuals is that they understand the process of internalizing success before it manifests. I've had the privilege to sit with some very successful men and women, and they all seem to share a common belief. Success has a lot to do with how much you will learn from those that know, and admit to what you don't know. You don't have the time to be egotistical or even prideful; success is no respecter of any of that jazz for which you have created a name. All those names were birthed out of a belief system you have adopted unconsciously that cause you to feel inadequate about what you didn't know.

A few years ago, I adopted a philosophy into the core of my existence. In this life I'm convinced, there are two kinds of people in the world. There are winners and potential winners who haven't gained the insight and know-how about winning. The winners that succeed in life have simply discovered their passion and infused it with desires to become what they believe they can be. It is a discovery that can happen at any point in life, but you have to be aware of it, so you don't miss the opportunity when it presents itself.

In many instances, it comes unexpectedly. A gifted person will become very familiar with their gift because it naturally unveils itself. However, through developing the environmental process of the gift, it will produce passion that triggers a desire to achieve it with a "no matter what" attitude. Whatever you are passionate about will drive you to the core of your belief until you achieve it. Your desire for a proper life should not be to 'scratch a hatch' but to unveil your true self.

Living your dream is the quickest way for you to experience life in ways that are extraordinary. Why is that? One reason that I have discovered is that it does not take much effort to be average. A person with dreams and goals must become someone who is intentional about bringing forth their best. It requires an unwavering amount of energy and faith. It is a process that calls for an exceptional desire to override the beliefs that have been instilled in you.

I will continue to show you throughout this book that there are two kinds of people in this life. There are those who have dreams with goals in mind and an ability to find ways to achieve them, and there are those that don't always seem to know anything about what's happening in their own lives. It simply looks like they exist in a body, but there's no life. They watch their lives pass them by, as they keep up with their daily routine.

On the other hand, you have those people who have a clear understanding of how they will fulfill their dreams. They have goals in mind, and they find ways to achieve them. They are fully able to commit and develop the habits of trust that create an allegiance between them and the pursuing of their dreams. These people also understand that you cannot commit to anything that you don't believe in and with individuals who don't.

An accomplished dreamer realizes that the process calls for you to start developing healthy habits.

One of those habits lies in learning how to celebrate small successes as well as significant achievements. They realize that it keeps the momentum going while working towards the major goal. Small wins have a way of multiplying when they are met with desire. There is something that happens in a person's heart when they can experience real success and be able to accomplish a goal or see a vision or dream come to life. It has a way of igniting confidence and trust that come because of faith in his or her God-given gift. I wish I could say that this holds true only on the positive side of things. However, desire also has a way of bringing challenges and struggles.

Most people realize that there will be some form of struggle or challenge that will occur for them to achieve their dream; however, for many, they fail to understand that the battle may extend to a longer period than they had imagined. If you are one of the people who took that leap towards pursuing your dreams and goals, you may be right here at this discovery point. It might be safe to say, "You understand what I mean." You may also have realized that the more you move towards your dream, the more strange events occur. It may cause you to question your dreams and if they are even worth pursuing.

It also causes you to ask questions like, "Is it worth the sleepless nights, or countless rejections?"

It seems like whatever could go wrong will go wrong, and it all happens when you are at that lowest point. I can think about the day when I was on an air-conditioning job at the height of the summer season. Prior to my being on the job, we had received a call from the customer complaining about her air conditioner blowing hot air. When I reached her home, the lady was so excited to see the quick turn-around time to her phone call. She had mentioned to me that her new granddaughter would be visiting the next day and so she needed to have the unit working. However, after checking the unit, I quickly realized that I did not have the part needed to fix her unit. Could things get any worse?

In further researching the part that was needed, I discovered that we didn't have it in stock. How would I tell this customer that she would probably have to be without cold air for another three days? Did you catch that? Have you noticed that when something goes wrong, it seems like everything else seems to goes wrong at the same time?

While busy taking notes at an event with my mentor, John C. Maxwell, I found myself writing down this quote, "Dream confessed creates conflict; dreams began to create a crisis."

"Dream confessed creates conflict; dreams began to create a crisis."

Wow. I had to pause to process what I had just transcribed and heard. In taking the time to analyze the quote, it was at that moment that pieces of my life's puzzle started making more sense and so this is what I came up with: the day that you decided on your dream and tried to move toward it, problems began to surface.

Instantly, as this reality hit me, I became discouraged. As I moved toward facing that reality, it was though someone had poured cold water right on my face. It became easier for me to understand why so many people give up. In all honesty, I was ready to give up. I honestly felt discouraged.

I get it. I have some idea of how you are feeling or how you felt. If you are not prepared for this reality, it is enough to stop you right in your tracks. Yet, I believe for you, it is, or can be, a different story. You, my friend, are part of the people who have taken or will take a different approach to making your dreams a reality. In being down this road several times in my life, here are some of the methods that may help you keep your momentum going:

- Develop a disciplinary lifestyle

- Be willing to do what other people won't do with a smile

- Keep your focus on the journey

- Often we tend to overestimate the event and underestimate the process

- Do what is necessary daily - not in one day

- Lao Tzu, the Chinese philosopher, has observed, "the journey of a thousand miles begins with one step."

- Become sensible to your behaviors

- Be intentional in your daily activities

- Celebrate small wins

- Remain engaged

- Take risks as needed with blind faith

I am confident that if you use all or most of these approaches, you will find that the path to your success will become much easier. You will begin to change the direction of your story. You will begin to allow your passion to drive you. You may even begin to recognize your desire to become an agent of change. The pursuit of fulfilling your dreams should not be based on luck because it is not a 'hit or miss' game.

The ability to fulfill your dream knows that when you work hard and act, there will be a win on the other side.

You should not only be thinking, if I can only get to the right place, at the proper time, in front of the right connection, but I could also have a chance to make this dream a reality.

One of the very significant things you need to be acutely aware of, to be successful in achieving your dream is that you cannot afford to live by mere chance. Throughout my life, I've never met any successful individuals that have ever moved to the top of the ladder by accident. They usually know what they must do and find themselves operating under the Nike slogan, "Just Do It." And that, my friend, could be an absolute challenge. Most of the people I know that have quit on their dream, only quit because they never expected to meet tough times throughout the process. Therefore, when the challenging times came, and they will come, it looked to be more than they wanted to bare. They allowed it to become the motivating killer of their dreams and desires.

My hope for you is that you do not permit these things to stop you. All you will be doing is denying yourself the possibility of creating the life you deserve. As you already figured out that life is not easy, and it will take a lot of effort on your part to achieve any goal. It will be painful at times, especially when all your hard work seems to be going nowhere. Do you know that sometimes being rejected by many and accepted by few can be a blessing? Rejection can be the critical point between you giving up, but don't let it.

Instead, allow your relentless pursuit, resiliency, and determination to a better life drive you through the pain of rejection.

Chapter 3:
My Dream Is My Ambition, But My Vision Is Of God

What Vision Are You Working Towards?

After almost ten years of doing life on my own terms, I walked into Abundant Life Christian Center, in Margate, Florida as a broken, lost, and confused young man. As I sat in the back of the church and watched this white-headed preacher stand before thousands of people to preach, these words rang out in my ear, "God loves you!" As he continued the message, I heard something that hit me like lightning, "God is a good God, He loves you, and He wants to bless you."

"God is a good God, He loves you, and He wants to bless you."

I didn't know, at the time, those words would set the mark for the journey of discovery towards my dream. For the first time, in my adult life, I felt a sense of hope. As I left the service, I didn't know what to make of it, but I allowed those words and the cool evening temperature to set my mind on those things from above.

I grew up with the mindset that some people were born to be blessed while others were born to live stressfully. For this reason, the message of God being good to all was at first confusing, but then it became very intriguing. All I knew about God is that you didn't play with him. Intrigued by the words of this white-haired man, I found myself going back for more. I was curious to know if I had ended up here by chance or was I at the right place at the right time for whatever unknown reason.

Up until this point in my life, everyone I knew was either going to prison or was being deported back to their homeland in Haiti, Jamaica, Dominican Republic, even Bahamas. I was afraid; I didn't want to be the recipient on either side of those outcomes, so I decided to keep going back for more. To my surprise, the message didn't change week after week. In fact, it didn't matter who was preaching, they each were saying the same thing. I was intrigued, and began to believe that this message must be right, but how would it work in my favor?

After almost two years of being consistent in attending service, on a Saturday night that was no different from most, something amazing happened that would be another defining moment in my life. Bishop Rick Thomas spoke a word over me. It was a word that would activate my dreams. He said as I stood there on the line with all these people, "big dreams" as he came in front of me. As he kept on moving, I replied in my head, "big dreams." I looked to the left and right thinking he couldn't be talking to me because I thought dreams were something that happens to you only when you fall asleep. For me, those were always nightmares not dreams, and there were always somebody chasing me or trying to kill me.

Anyway, as the Bishop walked back to me and put his hands on my shoulder he said,

"God says people will tell you, that you can't do this, you don't have the education, your skin color is not the right type, people like you don't do these kinds of things, your background is not the right type, but I am the one who will do this, sayeth the Lord."

These words have forever changed the course of my life.

Believe me, when I tell you, I tried to shake off those words, but I kept hearing the bishop's voice in my head. Why was this happening to me? I kept saying to myself, I don't have a dream and if I needed to have one where was I going to find it. As I struggled with this dilemma, the still small voice said so quietly it's within discovered it. I was already confused about life. Now I'm thinking; I'm losing my mind too. However, I obeyed by deciding I was going to allow it to come to me. I decided if it was within it would eventually show up.

The first thing I decided to do was to get involved with whatever the church had going on. I felt compelled to join a team that would call people and ask them if they needed someone to pray for them and prayed with them. On Friday and Saturday night, I would find myself in the back room in the church with a few others. We would be back there in a little room calling and

answering phone calls. We would talk with people who either wanted to add their names to the

prayer list or had some kind of issue they wanted someone to pray and agree with them. I must

admit this was not an easy thing for me to do giving the fact that English was my second

language. On top of that, I had never prayed with anyone in my entire life.

As I sat there sending and receiving calls, my palms would sweat, and my legs would

shake. I often found myself during that first night sitting down praying, "Lord Jesus, please let me make it through the evening without having to pray for anyone so I can at least see how it's done." Needless to say, he didn't pay me any mind with his incredible sense of humor.

I can remember, like it was yesterday, the very first call that came in. Yes, you guessed it right, it was my line that lit up, like a 100-watt light bulb. When I picked up the phone, the only thing I remember saying was, "Hello." I was so nervous and barely able to contain myself. It was, what I played out to be, one of the worst experiences ever. It was so bad that I purposely didn't want to remember what I had said to the person on the other end of the line.

Yet, something happened to me that night. I felt connected to something greater than myself, and kept going back. One night, I started talking to myself. I said something that went like this, "Pollo, why are you doing this to yourself? You will never get this. You are not qualified to even talk to yourself. What makes you think you can talk to other people you don't even know how to communicate? Stop embarrassing yourself." However, I wouldn't allow myself to give in to my fears and disqualify myself from the inheritance that belonged to me because I was on a mission. I was on a mission to find my dream.

Therefore, I switched the script and gave myself the reason I was qualified. Yes, I was a child of God, and all of his birthrights belonged to me.

He sent his servant to speak over my life, and I had chosen to believe and receive it. If anyone had strong enough reasons to walk away, it was me. In those days, it was a spiritual gift of mine to make excuses and create every reason why I shouldn't, wouldn't or couldn't. I am glad I endured the pain of not knowing how to discover how. A wise man once told me when you suspend the need to know how, the 'what' way will become clear.

I didn't know how to leave well enough alone. Out of curiosity, I chose to get involved with another group. In this group, I would go to the local juvenile centers and talk with young people. The very first day I started to speak, I felt the energy flowing through me. After a long day at my 9 to 5 job, I would find enough energy to go and talk to those young men in the center. I would feel this sensation of feeling empty even though I didn't understand at what point I had become full. Then I realized this was my sweet spot. I had a passion for teaching and inspiring people. Upon further reflection, I realized what the still, small voice I talked about earlier meant, and I did have a dream after all.

I began to embrace my reason for being alive was to teach and inspire. I had a dream, and now I was to focus on a vision to be in alignment with it. Do you know what I realized?

The more I shared my vision, the more clarity I had towards living out my dream.

Dr. John C. Maxwell says the following, and I couldn't agree with him more, "I want to make a difference, with people who want to make a difference, doing something that makes a difference, at a time that makes a difference."

Listen To Gods Direction For Your Dream

How do you listen to Gods direction for your dream? Over the years, God has brought some of the most incredible men in my life to mentor me. I recognize that I still have a lot of growing and a lot of areas where self-development is necessary. During this process, I have learned how to be mentored through great teaching materials from men like Bishop Rick

Thomas, Les Brown, and the late Dr. Myles Munroe. He played a major part in the discovery of my vision and my dream, especially after reading these series of books from him:

- *Understanding Your Potential-Discovering The Hidden You*

- *Release Your Potential Exposing-The Hidden You*

- *Maximize Your Potentials-The Keys To Dying Empty*

- *In Pursuit Of Purpose-The Key To Personal Fulfillment*

Power Of Vision

The more I sought clarity; I discovered another great man of God, John C. Maxwell. As a Certified Coach, Speaker, Trainer of the John Maxwell program, I have the privilege of being mentored and trained by him.

If you don't mind, I would like to pause right here so I can be completely transparent and honest with you. Even now, as I look back at the map of my life, if I had to map out my plan for success, I am not confident that I would have known where to begin. I am also convinced that the great leaders would not have been on my top-ten list toward my growth, and for many reasons. The first reason is that all of these men are out of my league.

The second reason being that my old circle of friends would never have exposed me to them. The God that I serve is an omnipotent God, and he knows better than me. God knew what I was going to need to help prepare me for the dream.

If there is anything in my life that I will never doubt is the unfailing love of God. He has proven to me time and time again that I can trust Him with my life.

Along the way, I developed systematic ways to listen more to this still, small voice. I create listening strategies as I embrace and grow into this person He is calling me to be. One of the things I started to implement is writing down what I was thinking. I know it sounds a bit foolish, but "God has chosen the foolish things of the world to confound the wise." I am learning to understand the difference between what I want, from what I desire.

By asking myself, "Do I want what I want for self, or do I want it for someone else?" The only agenda I have begun to focus on is whatever God is saying to me. This was the toughest transition for me. I am determined every day with great expectation to hear from God. I must admit that I often missed hearing the voice of God, which led to many mistakes because of the way I was expecting to hear from God.

It has required me to adjust my attitude, but it has been worth it. I also started visualizing what I was hearing, allowing it to bring me to greater clarity. I read the books in the Bible of how God spoke to people. One of the books I have found that speaks to that is Samuel 3:10-11. In this passage, God said to Samuel, "Listen carefully," and Samuel replied. "Speak, your servant is listening." Then the Lord said to Samuel," I am about to do a shocking thing."

Another verse that stood out to me is Psalms 40:6. It says, "Now that you have made me listen, I finally understand." Those verses have helped me to understand that God wants me to listen. He was not going to make me listen, and to me that is important. In knowing this, I had to make that decision in the matter. The next step would be a transition from listening to obeying and then learning how to trust God. There is no reason not to trust God.

There is no reason not to trust God.

Earlier, as I mentioned, He knew what was best for me; so He sent people in my life that would be a way to guide me. However, I knew that I would have to learn how to put my total trust in Him. One way I began doing this was by embracing that which was in the Word of God. I began seeking men in the Bible who trusted God. Abraham was one of those men, and in the book of Roman; chapter 4; Verse 19-21. The message shares how important it is to trust God while you wait on Him.

In going back to the book of Genesis, you will see how God spoke to Abraham concerning him, the father of many nations. However, his wife Sarai who would later be called Sarah seemed to be barren, and it caused him to ponder on how God's promise could hold true. Abram who later would be called Abraham would use his faith to believe that since God spoke it, then it would have to come to pass. It is through his great faith that Abraham would be known as, "the father of the faith." Even when there was no reason to hope, Abraham kept hoping and believed that he would become the father of many nations.

Abraham's faith did not weaken, even though, at about one hundred years of age, he figured his body was as good as dead. In fact, his faith grew stronger, and in this, he brought glory to God. Abraham was fully convinced that God was able to do whatever he had promised, and because of Abraham's faith, God counted him as righteous, according to Romans chapter 4; Verse 22. Do you know that Abrahams act of obedience, by remaining faithful, has been recorded throughout the Bible and registered for our benefit? It should serve as assurance to us that we hold fast to our righteousness, as we believe in the finished work or Christ Jesus on the cross and his resurrection.

Anyway let's move on. I am not here to preach to you, however, you may be wondering at this point, what does that have to do with you finding your dream? Well, based on science and the natural make-up of a woman, it is almost impossible for Sarah to have conceived a child outside her childbearing years. However, as Abraham found out, nothing is impossible with God. Yes, all the odds seemed to be against him and Sarah as they looked at the circumstances, but he knew that the God he served couldn't and wouldn't lie. Even when he might have thought about becoming discouraged, he remained faithful to the promise. In his faithfulness, Sarah, in her old age, gave birth to their son, Isaac.

Now, after hearing a snippet about Abraham's faith, are going to continue walking by faith? What will you continue to press toward until you see the manifestation of what God has promised? What do you believe in Him for? I have a good friend whose name is John Marquez, Sr. He is eighty-two years young and do you know what? He is still inspired to continue growing as a student of knowledge. He wants to make a difference in other people's lives, to which he refers to adding value to others.

John has spent most of his life competing with others instead of collaborating with others. In one of our meetings, he pointed out that, it wasn't until he started coaching with me that he saw collaboration was better than competing." I am grateful that he has given me permission to use his name and quote in this book. He also expressed to me, that for most of his life, he was dedicated to real estate, as a promoter of land development, housing, and apartment building. He was also the CEO of Overseas Sales and Investments Corp for more than two decades traveling, and enjoying every minute of it. He had offices in many countries in Central and South America.

John retired twelve years ago thinking that he was at the end of his life. However, by the grace of God, John said, "I am still very able and healthy at the age of eighty-two." Even at the age of eighty-two, John just now started thinking about creating a legacy that will benefit the younger generation. "Wow." It is a dream he has had for a long time, and is just now starting to pursue it. He has finally realized that he was not fully completed with what he was called to do while here on Earth. John still felt like his cup was half full.

As you can see, age is not something that should stop you from jumpstarting your dreams, but rather an engine to help you move your dreams ahead. It is never too later or too early for you to make progress towards accomplishing your dreams. Here are few fundamental principles you can use to start to begin the process:

- ✓ Think of what you want your life to be remembered for

- ✓ What can you do right where you are to kick start your journey?

- ✓ What are some things you possess and are grateful for?

- ✓ What do you believe about your potential?

- ✓ Raise the level of awareness of your natural ability.

- ✓ Take what you believe about yourself and your potential as God gifts to you.

The following were, and still are, some of the simple ideas I have used in my journey. In moving forward, you, too, must develop a system that fits you. It must be done in such a way that it keeps the candle burning. Often, when I meet someone for the first time, our conversation leads me to sharing my dream with him or her. I also end up telling them about my desires and my vision. Here is why I have chosen to do this:

Years ago, when I would meet people, I would ask them about their dreams they would show signs of unrest because they felt uncomfortable answering the question. I would even venture to say that they were embarrassed because they didn't know how to respond to the question. It was then that I realized that not everyone has a dream or desire and there are some who are uncertain about how to release it. As I have already confessed, I was one of those people, at one point, but since my encounter with God through my bishop, my projectile is different, and I am happy to share my dream, vision, and desires with others.

In sharing my dream with others, I see it as an opportunity to stir up the dream in others.

Too many people aim too low, and sadly enough, some don't aim at all. I love people, and I want to see them improve their way of life. It feels good to know that I played a part in helping others meet their goals. However, I found that the challenge is that more often than not, individuals who are making changes don't even realize it. They don't count it as credit towards the fulfillment of their dream or vision. For this reason, I invite them into my inner circle so that together they can learn to tap into their greater calling. However, they must become serious about tapping into that dream.

You will often find me telling people that there is no magic in having a dream, and you can't just wait for it to happen. It doesn't come to you; you have to go after it. It takes focus, dedication, and hard work. It will also mean creating a strategy.

I recently read an article from the publishing company, Think TQ. In the study they conducted in 2005, they identified how infrequently people develop a strategy for achieving their dreams. Based on the study:

- 26% focus on specific, tangible targets for what they want in life

- 19% set goals aligned with their purpose, mission and passion

- 15% write down all their goals in specific, measurable detail

- 12% maintain a clearly defined goal for every significant interest and life role, where they identify related daily, weekly, and long-term goals with deadlines

- 7% take daily action towards the attainment of at least one goal.

The study showed that fewer people are willing to take any significant action towards even the things they say they want to achieve, and that failure continues to be the result of not having a strategic plan in place to reach their aim or desire. To be quite honest with you, every dream needs a paradigm-shift. The only way you going to achieve your dreams is by doing the following:

- You must begin by saying yes to your desire

- You have to know and feel it's your God given duty to execute it.

- You must shift your belief system to trust in your potential as your right.

- You must remain a student of knowledge always looking for ways to grow and improve in the area of desire.

- You must be willing to lose, in order to earn.

The number one leadership guru, John C. Maxwell asserted, "Every dream is always rooted inside the dreamer, in his or her experiences, circumstances, talents, and opportunities."

You have a dream inside of you waiting to be given birth to, it's far bigger than you can imagine, it's a lot closer then you realize, and you are more equipped than you think to make it a reality.

Chapter 4:
A Dream Is A Process That Regulates Daily

What Daily Steps Are You Taking?

Personally, I hate the process because it is too much work and too painful. If you are anything like me, I have often wished, throughout my life, that I could have gone to bed, wake in the morning and found what I wanted had manifested. Unfortunately, according to the law of process, the road is not that simple. Benjamin Disraeli says; "The secret of success in life is for a man to be ready for his time when it comes." You cannot be ready if you don't allow the process to get you ready.

If you think that one day you will wake up and all of a sudden a completed dream will be lying in your lap, I will be the first one to tell you that you are going to be very disappointed because nothing worthwhile just happens. It is a process that you have to engage in from one day to the next, and for however long it takes.

The problem with most people is that they overestimate the importance of events and underestimate the power of the process.

This is a true story. I remember the day I came home and told my wife that I had an idea on how we could buy our first home. We had practically spent all of our money on our wedding, and needless to say, we were broke. We were living in a six hundred-square foot one-bedroom apartment. It was so small that the dining room, living room, kitchen, and the air conditioner unit all fit in the same space.

To save money, we decided, after a year of living in that small apartment, that it would probably be best for us to move in with her parents in their two-bedroom condo. We saw it as a great opportunity to save some money to buy a home then. Imagine how difficult this decision must have been. It takes a humble man to make such a move. Overall, living with my in-laws was not bad, but I was dying a thousand deaths every time I would drive to the condo, after a long day of work. It felt like I was less than a man.

We knew that it was part of the process. We stayed there until we managed to save almost six thousand dollars. I remember saying to my wife, Laurie, "Now we are ready to buy our home." You should have seen the look on her face. She looked at me like any supportive wife would. She then asked me the greatest question, "How are we going to do that babe?"

The question was relevant because she knew that we both had terrible credit and only six thousand dollars saved. At that point, I shared with her how I had met this lady who was a mortgage broker and a realtor. I went on to explain to her that the lady had told me that she could help us, but we would have to give her three thousand dollars to prepare some documents we needed to qualify for the house.

By this time, my wife just looked at me and said, "Ok." I was so excited, but I could sense that my wife was not as moved by the information. I know the whole situation seemed too good to be true, and it was. We ended up losing half of our savings that we had accumulated. I shared this story with a close friend who couldn't help but laugh. Although I was upset by the laughter, I've made a lot of dumb decisions in my life. I knew this was probably one of my most memorable stupid moves I made in my entire financial life, and what made it worse is that all the red flags told me it was a stupid idea. I ignored them all because I felt like it was (my spiritual gift to help speed up the process). I have learned a tremendous lesson from that experience.

I will say it again -

In life, there are no shortcuts. If you think you can cheat the process, you will find out the hard way, and instead of moving two steps forward, you will find yourself moving backward.

Don't misunderstand me. God can do anything He wants when He wants. He is a God of miracles but He does it with decency and in the right order, so He gets the full credit.

Here is what I have come to understand about life. It is a process everyone must go through. It is filled with ups and downs with losses and wins, which I prefer to call Wins and Learns, but the key is to learn from each one. I have never met anyone that enjoys having problems. As a matter of fact, every one of us, if we could have our way, would schedule nothing but good things for our lives.

I have also never met anyone of great success that didn't have to overcome some considerable difficulties. We can do everything we can to avoid having to experience bad things in our lives, but somehow bad things always seem to find us. My mentor, John C. Maxwell says in the twenty-one Irrefutable Laws of Leadership, "I try to take life one day at a time, but lately, several days have attacked me at once." Over the course of my life, it appeared that way most of the time. How has it been for you? In the journey to pursue your dreams, one of the things that can stand between you failing and success is the need to use shortcuts.

The earlier you realize that it is a process, the smoother the transition will be. Your dream is overloaded with good and bad, and often you will not be able to control it, but you should learn how to cope with it. In the midst of it all, you will still have to choose the quality of your attitude, and you must still display an attitude that will keep you on the winning side. My friend, your attitude will dictate the outcome. My advice to you is to maintain a positive attitude no matter what happens. For you see, as it is said, "Your attitude will determine your altitude," which emerges into conviction, and determines your belief.

A very wise mentor once said, "Going through the process of life is unavoidable and learning from it is optional. The choice is yours."

Your dream is meant to serve.

Who will your dreams benefit?

Do you know that your dream carries the ability and potential to make a positive difference in the life of the people around you? Dr. Hakeem says it like this, "Know when you serve others, you are fulfilling one of God's purposes for your life." For this reason, is it necessary for you to know your gifts?

One of the things I know is that I possess an abundance of passion for what I love. I am what most people would refer to as 'an introvert.' I am a very reserved person until you begin to talk to me about what I love. I have been identified as being an 'encourager' and 'inspiratory' as my sweet spot. I have found this to be my zone of strength. It is for this reason I am constantly looking for ways to add value to people in those areas of their lives. This might come across as being selfish, but this is the way I come alive and draw energy.

One of the things I have learned from my mentor is that the best way to add value to people is to put a ten on everyone's head when you first meet them. When you do this, you start off your relationship from a winning zone. When you take the time to look outside of yourself with a desire to help other people, it will influence how you look within. You see, we have been trained only to see what we are equipped to understand, and that is why two people can be in the same place, dealing with the same situation, surrounded by the same individuals, and see things in an entirely different way.

Let me take this time to share with you a story I heard about while growing up. It was a gentleman who lived on a farm. One day, a traveler came into town looking for a place to spend the night. The farmer offered him a place in his home to rest his head for the night. In the morning, the farmer woke up, as usual, with a cup of coffee, in his hand, and sat on the front porch. He did this routine on a daily basis before heading out to work in the field. As he sat on the porch, the young traveler came and sat next to him overlooking the vast land. The passenger felt compelled to ask the owner of the house what he was looking at.

The owner replied, "I see dry land full of dead trees."

After listening to his answer, the traveler turned and said, "Do you know what I see? I see a land with beautiful palm trees, beautiful houses with a bridge crossing from this town and leading into the next city."

I would call the traveler a visual-preneur. Although they both were looking at the exact same thing, their eyesight served them differently.

A long time ago, someone shared with me a story about a study that was done about two tables. One table was placed at an angle while the other table was set-up straight. They then asked a group of people if the tables were the same size. Every one of the participants in the group said that the straight table was longer. However, after the tables were measured, they discovered that all the tables were the same size. Not convinced, they again measured the tables, but their answer remained the same. As people, we tend to hold on to what we think to be true, regardless of what is proven because whatever we consider to be true becomes the thing that shapes our reality.

"The more a man thinks, the more he will understand, and the less a man thinks, the less his power of understanding becomes."

Not too long ago, I met a gentleman, whom out of respect, I will call Sir John. In a few of my initial conversations with Sir John, I learned about many of his achievements and successes in the real estate industry. As a realtor for over six decades, Sir John traveled the world. He opened and operated companies in places like Central and South America. He fluently speaks seven languages with an ability to transcribe many of them. Yet, as I have spent countless hours sharing with him principles learned from John Maxwell, Sir John would be the first to let you know that his belief system was incorrectly shaped by his false sense of reality.

At the age of eighty-two, he is now passionate about pursuing truth not through his distorted view, but based on principles that can be proven as truth through God's word. It has been my experience that far too many people, not even half of John's age, give up on pursuing knowledge because they think they are finished with learning. According to

www.mentalfloss.com/article/27590/who-reads-books

• One-third of high school graduates never read another book for the rest of their lives

• 42 percent of college graduates never read another book after college

• 80 percent of U.S. families did not buy or read a book last year

• 70 percent of U.S. adults have not been in a bookstore in the last five years

• 57 percent of new books are not read to completion

After reading about Sir. John, you might want to reevaluate your way of thinking and attitude towards life.

If you have ever felt like your life was no longer relevant, or perhaps someone has told you, that at your age, it was unnecessary to dream, or it was too late to push towards the mark of what you know is your calling, it is time to ignore it and keep on moving. The fact that you have made it this far in this journey, proven a lot about you and your commitment to living out your dream, I deeply hope you are taking these principles and my story into consideration. I can assure you that you are well on a pathway to separate yourself from those who say it's too late or too early to begin anything new.

A few years ago, while driving, I saw this bump sticker that read, "Dear past, thank your for all the lessons. Dear future, I am ready."

The way I see the future no matter the age is

I'm not where I want to be

I'm not where I'm supposed to be

However I'm not what I use to be

I haven't learned all I need to be, who I was born to be

I've just got to keep on learning how to keep going.

I always try to remind myself that I am a work in progress.

I don't need to learn it all in one day

As your friend I give this to you also. If you can embrace those words, like I have eventually your dream will be your reality.

Chapter 5:
Keep Your Dream In Perspective –

Which Perspective Will You Believe?

Often time, people grow up with the point of view of others such as their parents, community leaders, and the list goes on, and because we have lived in this way for so long, we begin to believe it. Parents and loved ones have great intentions, most of the time, towards helping their children in seeing the bigger picture; however, the problem often comes from them sharing their picture and not helping their children to discover theirs. We begin to identify it and even own it as ours. Yet, it is an act of our subconscious accepting it to be the truth because that is all we were taught. It then becomes our worldview affecting every situation in our lives.

If I may, I would like to ask you a question, "Do you believe that your dream is based on your perspective, or has your dream been influenced by others?" If it is, you are only ignoring your own desires and have chosen to accommodate the desires of others, be it parents, spouse, or peers. Although this may make them happy and may even allow you to be somewhat accepted by them to a certain degree, in most instances, it will not count towards the fulfillment of your dreams, and it will make it harder for you to attain success.

In your life, you must have a perspective that is clearly based on your dreams.

It is the responsibility of every individual to sort out his or her own life. As a matter of fact, when you opt out of other people's perspective and begin to adopt your own, you will find your dream. You will not only fulfill your dreams, but you will live the life for which God intended for you to live. It is a decision every one of us must make daily.

The question you may be asking yourself right now is, "When do you know you are pursuing other people's perspective?" Before I share with you some clues I have discovered, I would like to share another one of my stories. I remember when my mother would return home after going shoe shopping for my sisters, brother, and myself. She would call us to try on the shoes, but before we even attempted to put on the shoes, we could see just by looking at them that they were too big for our feet. I would put on one shoe and say," This is too big." Then she would grab some paper, stuff it in the shoes and say, "Try it now."

Like your dream, it doesn't matter how much you stuff it with the perspective of others, if it was not yours to begin with, it will not fit your purpose.

It will be nothing more than a weight you carry around and become irritated by, and any little thing will result in you being frustrated. You will be frustrated because you are outside of your dream and outside of the zone that you were meant to be in, doing it to please others and not yourself. Here are a few clues to help you recognize when you are pursuing other's perspectives:

1. Become aware of who is managing your worldview on critical subjects.

2. Find out what you believe concerning your own potential.

3. Find out what you believe about your ability to achieve a level of success.

All of us possess a natural ability known as 'the power of choice.' We can each think about what we want. Therefore, if you have been thinking from the perspective of others, you have a decision to make. You can either continue thinking this way, or you can make a conscious decision to change your thought process. You can move from what you know through experiences and challenges to what you can internalize because of your deeper revelation of understanding about your gifts and talents. Therefore, it will cause you to own a perspective about you.

Remember, everything you need to be successful has already been created for you.

The universe is waiting for you to be awakened to the absolute acceptance of this truth. It is the same intelligent ability that lives in every successful individual. It is just waiting for you to seek it and then unleash it. At this point, you must resist the desire to continue procrastination. You, my friend, must eliminate procrastination from your life, if you are ever going to enjoy it. Yes, it will not be an easy road, and there are many times that it may become unbearable, but if you are willing to practice a few simple disciplines daily, it will make the difference between winning and losing.

If you want to make the decision to recalibrate your way of thinking; if you are willing to change your circumstances and give your dream a chance to serve you, that my friend shows that you are stronger than you think, and for that, I must applaud you. Investment in self-growth is one of the greatest gifts you can give to yourself. Be careful because it does come with a price.

Throughout this journey, I had to pay the price of being criticized by the people that I love and respect. Ralph Waldo Emerson once said, "Whatever course you decide upon, there is always someone to tell you that you are wrong. There are always difficulties arising that tempt you to believe that your critics are right. To map out a course of action and follow it to the end requires courage."

Over the years, I have kept this quote close to my heart. It has benefited me greatly on my journey. It has also caused me to gain a few more of what we call "haters" because I have gotten to the point where I don't let what negative people say, matter to me. Although releasing it must be done, it does not make it any easier, especially when the hurt and criticism is coming from, as you may already know, the people who are the most important to you.

It is tough to have your dream criticized by people you admire, love, and respect.

I must admit this was a major weakness in my life; I had to come to terms that everyone who pursues a dream goes through criticism. I had to learn how to develop a thick skin attitude. I had to get to the point where I ignore them and not to listen to the opinions of untrained experts.

I don't know why some people feel like it is their spiritual gift to criticize others. However, if you want to achieve your dream, you must not allow misguided perspective of others to infiltrate your perspective.

In saying that, I must make this point here. Not all critics are wrong, but you need to learn when to pay attention and when not to listen to them. If the person or people who are criticizing you truly loves you and has pure motives without any personal agenda, then listen to what they have to say, especially if they continue to support you. However, if the individual or individuals are naturally critical of others, you may need to avoid anything they have to say because their opinion honestly does not matter. Criticism is simply one of the many things you will have to go through on the journey to achieve your dream.

Dreams are made only when people dare to try and are willing to pay the price towards their success.

Napoleon Hill, the author of "Think And Grow Rich" observed, "The fear of criticism is at the bottom of the destruction of most ideas which never reach the planning and action stage." A friend of mine once told me, faith sometimes begins by stuffing your ear plugs to ignore or block the noise trying to come in. Don't limit your possibilities to what you can see, don't listen to the noise; instead, identify with the voice behind the sound. Don't be controlled by what is logical. Believe that there is more to life than what meets the eye. Keep the image of the end in mind as you pursue your dreams, even when others can't see it happening and more so when *you* can't see it happening.

Everything around you is always moving; you too must always move to improve your ideal desires. The earth will not deny what it is you are seeking because everything you need to help you on this journey has already been provided. This is to be true, unless God contradicts Himself. Therefore, the desire to enrich your life by living out your dream is to enjoy a life created with your dreams and prompted by your actions.

Chapter 6:
Overcoming Impossibility Thinking

By now, have you gained some clarity surrounding what has kept you from moving forward?

Growing up in the streets of Fort Lauderdale we had street codes, such as "Snitches get starches," "Ride together or die together." As you get older, these kinds of thoughts become beliefs that drive your life. You either depend on people or blame people for your mistakes.

There may have never been a time in your life when you heard someone say, "You are responsible for your life. If you don't like what is happening in your life or environment don't try to change your circumstance, but change you." James Allen, the author of "As A Man Thinketh" said, "Men are anxious to improve their circumstances but are unwilling to improve themselves, therefore remains bound."

"Men are anxious to improve their circumstances but are unwilling to improve themselves, therefore remains bound."
- James Allen

I've experienced what Allen mansion here in this powerful quote, for years I felt trapped inside myself unable to do anything about my life condition, even though I was fully aware of my life choices was not one's that would benefit me. If I were to continue on that path because I didn't know what to do, I would make excuses or think this must be fate. I would never attempt to jump into the life I felt I deserved because of being afraid to take the leap of faith into the unknown.

Here's what I want you to capture here and that is you may not be fully aware of how the outcome will be. However, as long as you know, what you want the battle is half-won. The toughest decision you will ever face is to know what you want and act on it.

Someone asked me, "Why is it important to know what you want?" I spent half of my life, as a matter of fact, 20 years of my life struggling. Not because I was lazy or wasn't doing the right thing. I didn't have one job, in fact, I had three jobs. Trying everything to get by, but somehow just couldn't seem to make it, I got to a point in my life where I was tired. I wanted nothing to do with this kind of life.

I isolated myself from people that were sucking the blood out of me, so I started to hangout out with people that were ahead of me, admire them and mimic what I saw them doing. I was a hard worker, but it seemed that the harder I worked, the more broke I became. It didn't matter what I did - I just couldn't get ahead.

What I discovered, from my new circle of friends, was it is not working hard that got people ahead. If that were the case, every hardworking individual would be successful, but they're not. Some of the hardest working people I know are poor. You don't have to go to a foreign country to see this, for many of us, it's right in our own neighborhood.

It was not until that day when my mentor said, "The key to succeeding in life is to do things in a different way. You have to do things a certain way, and one of them is to start using the resources that are available to you."

Start using the resources that are available to you.

I began to read a significant number of books on self-improvement and leadership, applying whatever I was learning. One of my favorite motivational quotes come from the late great Earl Nightingale, who asserted or observed, "If you study a subject for one hour per day, then you'll be a national expert in five years or less."

How many of you read a self-help book, but never do the exercise in those books? "Guilty as charged." I've been there, but many pay thousands of dollars to a college institution to do those exercises. At the end of four years, they hand you a piece of paper, which states you are now certified.

I'm not against education, as a matter of fact, I consider myself to be a strong believer in education. However, our educational system has failed us, for most of us, if we like to admit it, we have been trained to believe that the way to become successful in life is only through a formal education. Some of the most successful people I know have very little education. Are they the lucky ones? I would like to think that people are successful based on their determination and desire to succeed.

I have a friend who dropped out of high school when he was 16 years old. In high school, he averaged D's & F's and his teacher told him it would be best for him to get a job. If he started early in life, he might make something of himself. Not only were his grades bad, but he also had a speech impediment.

After dropping out of school, he started to work for a roofing company. He hated it, but did it long enough to save some money and move to Florida where he decided to start his own cleaning business. A few years ago, he sold that company to start living his passion, and today my friend is a very successful entrepreneur.

My friend's story gives me courage every time I think of him because I grew up in an environment that teaches you that the only way to succeed is to go to school and get a job. In fact, that was the same advice I received from my Dad my entire life. We were never taught to go to school and become your own boss. When I was struggling to get ahead, I thought all I had to do was get my degree, thinking it would fix my life. I was wrong. The only thing my education did for me was put me into more debt.

Then I realized if I was going to change my circumstance, I needed to find a way to do that quickly, but how was I going to do that without a system or someone for me to imitate? I identified an opportunity to associate myself with people that were stronger, faster, and better than me. They were people, you could say, that were successful and I started to learn from them. As you probably have heard before, success leaves a trail and if that is true, I was willing to follow its trails.

Associate yourself with people who are stronger, faster, and better than you are.

One of the first things I realized was I needed to change my thought process. Successful people think differently. I had to change what I said to myself – successful people understand the power of self-talk. I had to change what I believed about myself – successful people believe in the power of positive affirmation. Successful people know what gets you there and what *won't* get you there.

For you to be successful, you have to break out of a poverty mindset. In order to get ahead and break out of your struggle, you have to literally, become a rebel against traditional beliefs, religious beliefs, and the educational system. As a matter of fact, these are the things that keep most people in a "lack" environment.

The thing(s) you lack in your life keep you thinking that it's outside of yourself and so you pursue it in other people. The reality is, it's all within you. You simply have to activate it.

Do NOT focus your energy on where you've been, and what you have or have not done. Instead, focus your energy on what you could do with what you have. This was the best decision I ever made. I began to figure out and know what I wanted and pursued it. As I began this process of knowing what I wanted for my life, the things I didn't want began to leave or exit my life.

I wish I could tell you that this process came without any pain but that was not the case. There were some people in my life I had to cut out and some things I had to give up. I became consciously involved in my own life and the more conscious I became, the more aware I became of the things that did not belong in my life.

It took me a long time to realize what I wanted, through many mistakes, because I did not know what I wanted. However, I did realize that everything I didn't want was occupying my life, but I was not even conscious of it. Looking back at my life's choices, I realized I didn't have a strong enough reason.

It has been said people are more likely to act themselves into feeling than feeling themselves into action.

When you have a good reason to do anything; nothing will get in your way. It's like the lion verses the gazelle in the jungle of Africa. Every morning, in the jungle of Africa, a gazelle wakes up. The gazelle knows one thing and that is it must run faster than the fastest lion or it will served up as lunch. Every morning, a lion wakes up. It knows that it must outrun the slowest gazelle or it will starve to death.

Both, the lion and the gazelle are running. The only difference is, one is running away from something and the other is running toward something. It really doesn't matter whether you are a lion or a gazelle; when the sun comes up, you had better be prepared to go after what it is that you want, whether you feel like it or not.

You cannot be successful in life if you don't know what you want, and be comfortable with what is going on around you. Victor Frankl, the writer of "Man Search For Meaning" said, "When we're no longer able to change a situation, we are challenged to change ourselves.

There are 4 main roadblocks that keep people from discovering their dreams. They are:

1. **Distractions** – A great mentor once told me, "Whatever does not help your progress toward achieving your dream goal, hinders it."

2. **Procrastinations** – this is the number one killer of most dreams. There will never be a better time than NOW to kick-start your dream.

3. **Traditions** – actually, this is the main reason for most people's failure. Tradition is a disease against growth because it has a way of maintaining things in the order it has always been. Tradition is an enemy of vision that could allow you to see further than your eyes alone can envision. Vision also believes there's always a better way. It dares you to try something new, while tradition keeps you in a safe and comfortable zone. To break the cycle of tradition, we have to move beyond the way we have always seen things.

I heard a story from the president of World Vision. It is about a family who was on a Carribbean cruise with a four-year-old girl. When they arrived in the middle of the ocean, the family decided to get on the deck. They were amazed as the looked at the vast endless beauty of the ocean. The little girl was unable to see a thing so she said to her dad, "I want to see," so the dad picks her up and put her on his shoulder. She took a deep breath and said, "Daddy look, look, look. Daddy look." The dad replied, "What?" She said, "Daddy, I can see further than my eye can look."

4. **Instant Gratification** - this is almost always the enemy of both progress and growth. We can choose to please ourselves and plateau or we can delay our gratification and take on the challenge so that we can develop and grow ourselves into a better future.

Here are some signs that indicate these enemies have affected your life:

1. Comparison - when you compare yourself with others, chances are, you'll allow yourself to be held hostage by your tradition(s).

2. Rationalization – you believe that there is good enough reason NOT to try

3. Isolation- some people withdraw for self-protection

4. Regret - a significant hindrance to living life in the present moment is regret.

5. Adversity - can make you better if you don't let it make you bitter

My great personal mentor, John Maxwell, says,

"To achieve your dream; you must embrace adversity and make failure a regular part of your life. If you're not failing, you're probably not really moving forward."

Chapter 7:
How To Win Against The Odds

Will You Dare To Be Different?

I will begin this section with two very life-changing questions. The first is, "What would you attempt if you knew you would not fail?" The second is, "How would your life be if you had nothing to fear?" According to the Merriam Webster's Dictionary, fear means to be afraid or apprehensive. Did you know that fear has robbed many individuals of their best years of their life? Why is that? Well, one reason is that people are afraid of failure. They are scared of being rejected. They don't want to be seen making a fool of themselves. Yet, when we look at people of significance like Oprah Winfrey, Michael Jordan, and Arnold Schwarzenegger, you will find that their years of successes has been coupled with many years of failure.

Fear is a part of all of us. Don't be fooled. Fear is as real as your next breath.

Fear is a part of all of us. Don't be fooled. Fear is as real as your next breath. However, no one has ever achieved anything worthwhile without fear. This tells me that most of us have more courage to overcome fear at any point in our life. Not all fear is bad. The reverential fear of God is good. It is the kind of fear that causes us to reverence a God who gives us the ability to dream. Your dream is not a mistake, and His purpose for your life will overcome your fears. It is your responsibility to outlive your fears. It is your duty to get to your destination, regardless of how scary it may seem to you.

You possess a gift that the world needs. Your fear qualifies you for what you were born to do, so don't minimize it nor maximize it; instead, you need to use that fear to advance you to your greatest level. One of my hero's of the twenty-first century is Nelson Mandela. After being released from prison, he said, "I learned that courage was not the absence of fear, but the triumph over it."

I now see fear as nothing more than a process to activate my journey to living out my dreams. You can't buy into fear, and you can't let it stop you from reaching your dreams. You can either choose to overcome your fears by doing what it takes to enjoy life, or you can decide to let it keep you in that place where you live a very mundane life.

You can either choose to overcome your fears by doing what it takes to enjoy life, or you can decide to let it keep you in that place where you live a very mundane life.

The UCLA Coach, John Wooden says, and I quote, "Things turn out best for the people who make the best of the way things turn out." Recognize what you have to be grateful for and focus on that. No fear can stop God's destiny for your life; only you can do that. Step out and dare to make a difference. Take a look at the following suggestions from my mentor, John C. Maxwell:

- "If there were ever a time to dare, to make a difference, to embark on something worth doing, it is now. Not for any grand cause, necessarily but for something that makes your heart jump. Something that energizes your aspiration. Something that makes your dream believable.

- You owe it to yourself and the rest of the human race to make your time on this earth count.

- Have fun - dig deep - stretch and dream big

- Know, that nothing worth doing seldom comes easy.

- There will be good days. And there will be bad days. There will be times when you want to turn around, pack it up, and call it quits. Those times tell you that you are pushing yourself and that you are not afraid to learn by trying.

- I've heard it said many times there are two great days in everyone's life: The day you were born, and the day you discover why.

- Seek after what God has put you here to do.

- And go after it with all of your heart as if your life depends on it, because it does."

To be what you want, you have to know what you want.

Think about something that you would like to achieve. Do you have a clear picture of it in your mind? I want to share with you some principles I've used that help me to kick-start my life in the direction of my dream.

Most people I know have dreams. My rich friends have dreams, and my poor friends have dreams. Sadly, negative people have dreams, and positive people have dreams or something they would like to see come true that would change the world, but fail to capture exactly the kind of change they want to see happen, therefore it remain nothing more than a wish.

Before you can change anything, you must understand what it is that you are going to change. Nothing changes unless you change. First, the days I heard my personal mentor John, speak those words, it was like manna from heaven.

The most common question I get from people about dreams is, "How do I know exactly what dream to focus on when I have so many ideas fighting for my attention?"

Create a clear definition of your dream:
Dreams are not supposed to start with reality. They are supposed to be fantastic, incredible, and birth out of desires, hope, and possibilities:

- o Dreams are a product of imagination and creativity
- o Dreams are the product of your beliefs
- o Your belief is the product of your thoughts
- o Your thought produce for your beliefs
- o Your belief emerged into conviction
- o Your conviction determines your attitude
- o Your attitude dictates your perception
- o Your perception create your character
- o Your character show up in your behavior

Here are some of the reasons why it's so important to know exactly what you want. In order to help you, here are some practical steps to consider:

Step One - Answer The Following Questions:

- ➢ What do you like to do?

➢ What are your gifts, talent, abilities and personal vision for yourself?

➢ Is there something that strangers tell you that they see in you?

➢ Do you come alive when you talk about it?

The word "stranger" is used on purpose meaning people who have no invested interest on either your wins or loses, but can see your passion when you talk about it. This attitude has nothing to do with skill set. You may know a lot of skillful people who are not talented, and some talented individuals who don't possess an ounce of skill. Let me explain.

For you to reach the mastery level of your talent, it has to intertwine with your gift, as well as your ability.

For you to reach the mastery level of your talent, it has to intertwine with your gift, as well as your ability. Sadly, most people don't reach that level of mastery because they're not willing to make the sacrifice required to get them to the level they deserve.

Now let's say that you're gifted in the area of basketball, but you have to have enough humility to allow someone that may not even be as good as you are to mentor or coach you through a process. You can learn the fundamentals of the game such as how to play with other people, stay in shape, practice tiredly to improve on your technics that doesn't require talent or a gift. All you need is ability and discipline.

For example, Allen Iverson one of the most controversial basketball player of all time, according to his biography, he played for the Philadelphia 76rs. Now Allen's problem wasn't his controversial behavior, he simply was un-coachable. He wasn't showing up for practice because he thought his game was sweet, but despite this, no one can deny his talent. He was a beast.

Since he didn't develop discipline, it cost him more than he would like to admit. He was a very successful ball player. If you ask anyone, they would most likely agree. Allen had the skill, talent, ability and potential to be great, like Kobe. In fact, he could be greater, but he failed because he lacked the key ingredient that makes one a legend which is discipline. It doesn't matter how successful you are. If you lack discipline, regardless of how talented or skillful you are, you will never be great.

If you lack discipline, regardless of how talented or skillful you are, you will never be great.

Step Two: Keep A Journal

Write down your dreams and the reason why you want them to be a reality. Also, what are the things you would be willing to do to achieve them? Think of everything that could (possibly) go wrong as you go after your dream. Will you be mentally prepared for the unexpected when it comes?

Step Three: Set Specific Goals For Your Personal And Professional Life

You need to have a specific set of goals for both your personal and professional life. What is a goal?

- A goal is an established point of achievement that moves you to a greater accomplishment.
- A goal is a point of measure for progress toward your purpose.
- A goal is a prerequisite for the achievement of an ultimate plan.

Recognize this:

- ➢ Goals shape plans
- ➢ Plans shape action
- ➢ Action achieve results
- ➢ Results produce success

Every human being should have a set of goals to achieve, one way or another. Even the individual who's failing at life is setting goals that cause him to fail.

As a matter of fact, many of us unconsciously live our life *not* doing things that would cause us to be successful. We don't set up goals or do the things we truly want, love, or even care about. This causes us to follow someone else's plan or we end up setting the wrong kind of goals. Wherever you find yourself in life, it is a result of the goals you have set or the ones you choose not to set.

Wherever you find yourself in life, it is a result of the goals you have set or the ones you choose not to set.

How Do You Go About Setting Up Your Goal(s)?

You have to plan for them realistically. Ninety percent of people who set up goals, almost always, without fail, never achieve them because they are not realistic about setting them.

They don't set them in the proper sequence with the possibility of not reaching that goal, due to issues outside of their control. They also fail to recognize setting up goals is not about accomplishment but about tracking progress.

This is why I recommend:
#1 - Be realistic about your goals and
#2 - Set them with "if" in mind.

A positive-thinking, self-motivated guru would tell you if you do that, you're doubting or contradicting yourself. I don't believe that at all. As a matter of fact, when you do doubt or contradict yourself, you are protecting your sanity and preventing giving up altogether when things don't turn out to be the way you expected them to be. This way of thinking will help you find new ways to do things differently.

Family

When it comes to your relationship with your family, how much time are you going to dedicate to spend with them on a weekly basis?

It has been said time and time again that no one ever comes to the end of his or her life and wishes they had more money, prestige, or worked harder. However, people always say they wish they had spent more time with their loved ones.

Friends

Is there a friend that you need to cut out of your life because they are not advancing your growth? Keep in mind if you hang out with nine broke people, you are bound to be number 10.

Health

Take a moment to seriously consider the following questions:

✓ Are you out of shape?

✓ What food(s) do you need to avoid?

✓ How often do you exercise?

✓ How can you improve your eating habits?

✓ Who will be responsible for holding you accountable?

✓ Do you have health issues that need to be addressed?

Setting up goals and sticking to them is a huge milestone toward achievement and success, but the rewards produce happiness, a healthier lifestyle, and more fulfilling relationships, plus you can sleep better at night.

Step Four: Look At Your Options

This is a critical part of the process for getting to your destination.

A wise man once said, "If you're building a house you are to count the cost first before you start building, otherwise, you will not be able to finish the project."

You have to know who your source is before you go out looking for resources.

#1 -The first thing you must know is that you are your resources.

#2 - Keep your eyes and ears open for intuitiveness and listen

#3 - Exhaust all of your resources before looking for outside resources

There are people that have been assigned to help you achieve your goals and dreams in life and are searching for you. My question is to you is - What options are you giving them in finding you?

Step Five: Failure Is Part Of Success

It has been said that past failures are one of the main reasons that stop most people from taking risks or to go after their dreams. Failure is important to your success because you cannot succeed at anything unless you have failed at something at least two or three times.

Failure is not your enemy; you can pull from them "lessons learned" so that you don't repeat them. Let the past be the past because you cannot change the past.

Failure is not your enemy; you can pull from them "lessons learned" so that you don't repeat them. Let the past be the past because you cannot change the past.

Refusing to allow your experience to classify you as a loser though you may have had some major pitfalls will reward you awesomely in the future.

Step Six: Is There A Voice In Your Head?

What voice(s) are you listening to? Are they voices of others or your own intuition? This is a point where your best friend or family members can become your enemies, and this is the only time I would probably tell you that it's okay.

In the book, "Think And Grow Rich," the author, Napoleon Hill, made a statement that has impacted my life. He said, "The majority of people permit relatives, friends, and the public at large to so influence them. They cannot live their own lives because they fear criticism." It's interesting how some people become angry when you step out and start to do what they have never done.

I often tell people who don't take criticism well, "Do not ever listen to the opinions of an untrained expert."

Some friends do not want you to 'break out of your situation' because they don't want to feel left behind. You have to accept that and keep moving whether they support you or not. They are not your source. The only voice that should override your own is God's.

Often we get caught up in the rat race comparing ourselves with other people successes. I want to encourage you to learn from as many people as you can, but try your very best to be the best version of you.

Step Seven: Do You Allow Success To Stop You From Growing?

Often people reach a level in their lives where they're comfortable experiencing a little bit more than they used to, enjoying life with the one they love without financial burdens, and stop growing. The result is detrimental to their success. Success is a great way to encourage your progress but that does not mean you're at your destination yet. Sadly, many people stop growing after they have tasted success.

Success is a great way to encourage your progress but that does not mean you're at your destination yet. Sadly, many people stop growing after they have tasted success.

We are never where we should be because there's always one more level, we can reach one more goal in life. There is always one more challenge we can overcome. We haven't learned it all to arrive at the level of mastery. We must learn to keep on going and reach for our highest calling. We must keep on stretching until we're all stretched out like a rubber band.

The greatest enemy of tomorrow's success is today's success. The major difference is the gap between good and great, so how do we close that gap? Are you willing to stretch?

Robert Louis Stevenson said, "To be what we are and to become what we are capable of becoming is the only end to life."

Step Eight: Take Action

The essence of success is not in what you know; it's in the bias attitude for action(s). You have to believe that you can make a difference. Every person on this earth – including you and I – has the potential to make a difference. We can only do it when we take action(s). This does NOT mean taking foolish action, but nothing can be accomplished if we don't take any action at all.

Taking action is a very sensitive subject for many people. Here's what I mean; some people have no trouble doing what others may think is crazy, like jumping off a plane. You couldn't pay me enough money to do that because I know I wouldn't live to enjoy it. The fear of height alone would kill me, however for someone else, it is a thrill.

Action must be evaluated not by the fear it generates in you or the probability of your success, but by the value of its outcome.

Chapter 8:
Realizing Your Goal

When you have achieved anything worthwhile, you have probably subconsciously or consciously realized your goal or objective. Having a specific goal helps you stay focused on your specific purpose. They can serve as 'reminders' or incentives as you pursue your goals and dreams. Goal setting is widely used by individuals in business, top athletes and high achievers. It can involve a more formal process for personal planning or a career, but getting in the habit of setting goals allows you to do the following:

- Stay focused

- Determine what is important for you to achieve in your life

- Know what you must concentrate on to achieve your goals and dreams

- Helps prevent distractions

- Provides both short-term and long-term motivation

- Get and stay organized

- Track your progress

- Develop a level of self-confidence and competence

Many times, you will need to create sub-goals and tasks under larger goals that involve breaking down smaller tasks and targets that will help you reach your long-term goals.

Many times, you will need to create sub-goals and tasks under larger goals that involve breaking down smaller tasks and targets that will help you reach your long-term goals. Make a plan and then work your plan. Create an intentional statement that will empower you to keep on moving forward toward your goal.

Set A Precise Goal

Goals should have qualities that are specific and measureable so you can see exactly what you have achieved. For example, use dates, amounts, time, or anything that helps you determine and know what exactly you must do to achieve your goal. Break it down into smaller steps and tackle each step in a consistent manner. Be realistic, however by keeping goals small and incremental for each step, it will give you the opportunity for a reward.

Include target dates and time lines that will provide motivation to continue your work until the situation or problem is solved.

This activity will also help you place a time limit on how long you are willing to wait for an appropriate response to your efforts and work. Give each goal a priority, as this will prevent you from feeling overwhelmed by having too much to do. You can give your proper attention to the most important steps to achieve as you move toward your long-term goal. Find that happy medium meaning setting goals that are not too high, but not too low either. Setting goals that are just slightly out of your immediate grasp will still give you hope in achieving them.

Using Your Goal Setting Worksheet

Before you start on your Goal Setting Worksheet, take some time to analyze your goals. For example, you might want to list the advantages and disadvantages of achieving a specific goal. What are the benefits? Are their key steps that you must take to achieve your goal? When will you be able to do these specific steps? Record deadlines and dates for each step.

List any resources that will help you along the way, such as contacts, money, and time.

List any resources that will help you along the way, such as contacts, money, and time. What are the outcomes? In other words, did you achieve each step? Take some time to reflect on what you have achieved.

List Your Achievements:

1.

2.

3.

4.

5.

Goal Setting Worksheet

Goal Statement

How will this goal benefit me?

What steps are needed to achieve the goal?

What timeline is there?

Who can help me achieve this?

What obstacles are there?

What solutions are there?

Who would be responsible for keeping you on track?

How would you celebrate your progress?

I will have this goal completed by

Signed _____

Date _____

Chapter 9:
Work Your Plan

Don't leave the circumstances or story of your life to chance. If you want to achieve personal and professional success, following the steps in this book will help you get where you want to go. Everything we do in our daily life including our jobs from making breakfast in the morning to helping your child solve a math problem, involves specific steps in the process. Each step must follow a specific order if the process if you are going to achieve the desired results.

Frankly, our entire lives are one long, continuous process comprised of individual steps.

The long-term processes may be a bit more flexible than others, however we can rearrange the steps as needed throughout our life and career to reach our goals. Either way, we still need a plan to follow if we are going to achieve what we desire.

Challenges To Be Aware Of In Developing Key Performance Indicators

Your mind may be racing with ideas for setting your goals and what you want to achieve, but it takes considerable effort to develop a good set of key performance indicators that measures their importance. Here are just some of the challenges you need to consider. Answer the following questions:

Are your objectives clear?

Are you focused on just financial outcomes? Relying solely on financial indicators can give you an incomplete and unbalanced view of the health of your goals and objectives.

Are there measures that you deem important but others do not?

Are there any conflicts of interest?

What areas of your goals or objectives need to be revised or revisited? Sometimes, it takes a fine-tuning process and time by all parties involved to address any issues that arise.

Using your key performance indicators involves a regular review to assess the meaning of the results you are achieving:

Are the results positive or negative?

What can you do to improve and strengthen any of these areas?

Have any conditions deteriorated? If so, why?

What actions can you take to improve future results of your objectives and goals?

Taking time to answer the questions above can act like instruments or tools that work together to give you a total picture. It is like checking the weather report before heading out on a boat or trip. You get a clearer picture of your total situation and what you can expect. You can develop your own personal scorecard like the one developed by Dr. Lauchlan A. K. Mackinnon at thinkdifferently.org. It is based on a balanced set of criteria for personal growth and performance.

Why Do You Need A Personal Balanced Scorecard?

As a life coach and consultant, our approach to success is not always balanced. We may focus on one area only, such as our career or attaining wealth, and neglect other important areas of our life such as relationships or our health. You might be thinking, "Oh yes. The work-life balance that we all need to achieve." While it sounds good, it does have some problems and issues. It doesn't lead you to think about and identify exactly what is important to you. Plus, it does not provide an indicator of how well you are progressing against all other things that are important to use in your life.

Develop Your Personal Performance Management Scorecard

You can build your own personal performance management scorecard by assessing what areas of your life are important. It may be different for each one of us, as an individual. For example, your scorecard might include spirituality, health, relationships, career, finances, or your life purpose. You then can assess where you are currently in relation to each of those areas, such as where you would like to be or if you have achieved the ideal situation, and what your current objectives are for that area. Here are the steps to developing your Personal Scorecard:

Define The Areas Of Your Life That Are Important To You

This is a huge step. The list you build will be different for everyone and should include the core things that are central to your life. Ideally, you will have at least 15-20 areas of your life identified such as where you live, your financial situation, the level of connection to God, the love in your life. Here is a list to get you started:

Career

Financial situation

Romantic relationship

Family

Health and Fitness

Spirituality

Life purpose

Social life

Personal Growth

Satisfaction

Positive impact on the world

Travel

Life experiences

There are all sorts of areas in your life that may become more important to you as you experience growth and success, such as passion, freedom, or contentment. Do these ring a bell? Use the chart below to write down the areas of importance on the left side

Area	Current Status	Ideal	Measure	Goal	Action

You can adjust the list until it feels right to you. For each you list, evaluate honestly where you are. How do you feel about that area? On the same note, be proud of what you have accomplished and appreciate the good you have and are doing in your life at this moment. When you have an area that needs improvement, make a note and describe how you feel things could be better. Get a journal that will give you more room to write or create a document in your computer.

As you review each area of your life from where you would like to be, describe your visions for each one. Be creative. Include the impossible and write it down in the "ideal" column. Do you need to add new areas in your life? In going through this process, you may have found some surprises, areas of your life that you have taken for granted, and some areas where you have new developments and goals.

Chapter 10:
Develop Your Measures

For each area of your life, how do you know when you have it? Is there a quantity or quality that you can track your success? For example, if your financial goal is to make more money per month, how are you doing in this area? Or perhaps it is qualitative where you have a consistent feeling of high-level connection with your spouse.

For example, if you achieved more financial success, does that give you more security, confidence, power or freedom? Make your measures emotionally meaningful to you. If one of your areas includes losing 20 pounds, while that is specific, it might be more meaningful for you to fit into a favorite suit, pants or jeans making you feel more empowered.

Identify Your Specific Objectives

In the "goal" column, you want to start with something specific and measureable. For example, instead of saying you want a new career, say something more specific such as "I want to be a Writer for a large publisher with a salary of $85,000 per year." Expand this goal even more by asking for a bigger salary or being able to travel with your spouse or a friend. What is it about this position that appeals to you? Is it the travel? Writing on your own? Getting into the publishing world?

What Is The Most Important For You To Achieve?

What are your important goals right at this moment? What are you passionate about? You certainly cannot achieve all your goals all at once. Focus on the one that is most important to you. Perhaps choose three or four goals to work on and break them down into smaller tasks.

Write down your action plan for each of these areas that you want to achieve. You now have your personal strategy map.

Work Your Plan

In pursuing your current goals, check back periodically to see how your efforts are impacting a specific area and other areas of your life. You can do this on a weekly basis to see if you need to make any changes. In addition to monitoring your progress as you work your plan, you can check back or revisit the entire process on a regular basis – perhaps quarterly or every six months.

Key Indicators

In addition to using your strategy map, you will find it useful to develop some key indicators that will help you monitor your progress and growth. These can vary for each person, but you may want to determine if your goals are challenging enough or how effective you performance has been. If you are so inclined, it would be wonderful to hear from you about your experiences, how useful this process has been for you and what you would like to change in your life.

In working your plan of action, it will help ensure that the steps in the process are in the right order. In summary, it is a 5-step process that includes the following:

- ✓ What is your dream?
- ✓ Create your purpose statement
- ✓ Develop specific goals for each area you defined

✓ Measure your progress

✓ Take Action

It boils down to the ultimate goal that you set for yourself. Your vision(s) should reflect a long-term view and remind you of who and what you want to be, both professionally and personally. It is what drives you each and every day. Do you have a mission statement for yourself? "Live peacefully and happy" or "Be true to yourself."

Let go of anything inauthentic and all activities that do not mirror your highest intentions for yourself.

When we open our hands and release unhealthy situations to God, divine power can enter. Miracles always follow when we surrender troubling conditions. You will find that the relationship, job, health issue, or other circumstance heals rapidly in ways you might not have ever imagined. You can expect a miracle when you decide to be true to you.

Have courage to live a life that is true to your heart, not the life others expect you to live.

Think BIG. Create your mission statement that perhaps summarizes your intentions and how you will achieve your mission for each area of your life. It should simply and quickly describe what you do and who you are. You can turn the impossible into the possible. Make your vision a reality by being clear about the outcome you want to achieve. Your goal should inspire you to take action.

As the writer Thomas Merton once said, "Happiness is not a matter of intensity, but of balance, order, rhythm, and harmony." If we focus too much in one area, other areas of our lives will suffer. Create goals that are specific to the different areas of your life. Remember that the purpose of your goals is to move you closer to your overall vision. If there is a discrepancy between your vision and your goals, then you may need to make some adjustments so that your goals align with your vision. Track your progress daily or weekly using a chart, chalkboard or a software program that will allow you to track your progress. It should clearly display all of your goals and your progress toward achieving each one.

Make sure it is easy to update. If not, it will be too difficult to maintain and you will simply give up. Be consistent and having your information across multiple devices can be quite helpful. You can save various versions and compare them as you go. Choose a day of the week where you have some time to reflect on your goals and see how you are performing. Do you have a plan of action such as a weekly schedule for working on the goals in each area of your life?

Don't feel bad if you miss a goal. Figure out why you did and then take specific steps to achieve your goal that will get you back on track.

You must allocate time to work on your goals in order to achieve them.

I realize this is not easy with family, job, school and professional responsibilities, however creating a schedule that you can adhere to will help you be proactive.

Find a **mentor or a coach** that you trust to guide you and with whom you can share your goals and dreams. Does this person have a genuine desire to help you improve? Allow this person to help you find opportunities to achieve your goals. Share your goals with everyone you meet and talk about what you want to achieve. By doing this, we can open up to other people and gain insight into how you can help each other be successful.

Using Your Plan For Success

Your strategic plan is NOT a one-time creation that you set aside and forget about. It requires regular attention by you. Review it often and make sure you follow the schedule that you have established. Depending on your situation, you may spend an hour per day or a couple of hours each month to update your progress and focus on your vision. Ask yourself:

What have you learned?

What touches both your heart and emotion?

What will you do differently?

What skills do you still need to develop or improve upon?

Adjust your goals and make sure you continue to require that you do your best. This will help you make concrete progress. Be specific. Having a strategic plan will help you balance both your professional and personal goals, create order, evaluate your decisions, and reduce any risk that will support your future success. It will help you determine which is the right path to take in all aspects of your life.

Your plan will not only help shape your future, but help you be confident in achieving the goals in life that matter to you the most.

Final Thoughts

Not having a dream was a source of my confusion. It was not until Bishop Rick Thomas spoke those words prophetically over my life did something happen. Those words caused my dream to move like a volcano from dormant to active. In retrospect, I would say that I did have a dream. However, I never had allowed that dream to manifest. Instead, I was too busy listening to all the negative chatter.

I was too busy paying attention to not having enough education, not being the right skin color, not growing up in the right family, or not having the right background. This was an idea I fought because I couldn't figure out how this would even be possible? But what I lacked was the main ingredient, "Not by might nor by power but by my spirit," sayeth the Lord.

My dream could only come to life when I began to understand that my purpose for living was to complete his purpose for giving his only begotten son.

The fulfillment of my dream became active when I would allow my impossibilities to live through his limitless possibilities.

Believe me, when I tell you, I tried to shake off those words, but all I kept hearing was my bishop's voice. Why was this happening to me? I kept repeating over and over again, I don't have a dream, but "He" had a dream for my life. It took the prophetic voice of my bishop to bring life to my bones, and that has been the prophetic word that I lived by for more than five years.

I began to use those words to speak life to help me bring forth my dream and pursue my destiny. I've come to realize the things we speak and confess to create the condition of our existence. You may have heard it said; "What you think about you bring about." If you think you are a winner, you probably will win most of the time, and if you think you are going to lose, you have already lost every time. Whatever you speak into your life long enough becomes prophecy and will determine your destiny.

What Will You Speak to?   I believe in you. Your best days are not outside of yourself but within you, waiting to be exposed.

May God's Grace Empower you as you embark on the journey of discovery to your dream and to live the life you were meant to live.

I Love you and will see you on the other side of your dream.

Connect With Pollo

At what point in this book did you realize you have been working toward a dream? The author would love to hear from you about how this book inspired YOU. Contact:

pollo@prosperinspires.com

About the Author

Pollo Prosper is a Certified John Maxwell Coach, Trainer, and Speaker. He is the founder of Prosper Inspires Consulting, LLC, a company dedicated to providing leadership resources for leader shift transformation to help individuals and businesses reach their personal and professional potentials. Pollo currently resides in the beautiful City of Boynton Beach, Florida.

As a leadership expert and Coach, Pollo works with companies that appreciate the value of personal development who want to build a stronger team by developing their leadership skills.

His journey has not been one where you would say he had a chance to win because the odds were greatly against him given his circumstances. Growing up on impoverished islands of the Caribbean, on the isle of Haiti, coming to America was not any different for him to say the least.

Daily survival was often a struggle and intensified, as he had no father figure in his life. His language became one of his largest growth barriers. People who took drugs, smoked everything under the sun, and drank alcohol always surrounded him. Yet, he thanks God that his life was not affected by those influences which to this day, he has never engaged in.

There are thousands of individuals like Pollo who have experienced great hardship in growing up and yet he is very sympathetic towards them, especially because of the early part of his life journey. One's beginnings do not have to determine your present and future. He is a living testimony of what a little determination and a lot of hard work can do. His goal and passion in life are to help others to live their best life. He wants to see people reach their full potential.

For More Information, please contact:

Pollo Prosper

John Maxwell Certified Coach, Trainer, and Speaker

Web: www.polloprosper.com

Email: pollo@prosperinspires.com

Office: 561-320-1539

Cell: 954-892-4337

Coaching Services
Individual or Small Group Coaching

Do you want to create the quality of success in your career or your personal life that generates the financial freedom that makes you tap dance to your Journey of life? If so, and if you are willing to take action, there has never been a better opportunity than now to act, and you've come to the right place. I can help, I work with people just like you who are in a job or career they don't like and help them to reach their personal and professional potentials.

Customized Seminars and Workshops Training

- How to overcome impossibility mind-set

- Success factor the ability to connect with others determine the height of your

  potential

- Life's greatest lessons are gained from our losses

- Being busy isn't the same as being productive

- Make every day of your life matter

Pollo is available for Keynotes:

Conferences (nationwide, regional, state or local

Meeting any time of the year

Incentives trip gathering

Sales Training

In-house presentations

Public Seminars

Leadership Gatherings

Any other function where an (outside) speaker is feasible

Call or email today to learn more about these customized programs

Office: 561-320-1539

Email: pollo@prosperinspires.com

Website: www.polloprosper.com

RESOURCES

John C. Maxwell Quote: Intentional Living Chosen A Life That Matters. First edition October 2015 published by Hachette Book Group, INC.

ThinkTQ.com; http;//www.thinktq.com/training/article_artical.cfm?1364A81D073.

The Holy Bible, NIV The Zondervan Corporation Zondervan.com (p)

John Wooden Quote: SuccessAcademy.com

John C. Maxwell Quote: PUT YOUR DREAM TO THE TEST
Published by, Thomas Nelson, INC.

https://www.uky.edu/ ~eushe2/Pajares/OnFailingG.html

NOTES

NOTES

NOTES

NOTES

www.ingramcontent.com/pod-product-compliance
Lightning Source LLC
LaVergne TN
LVHW081318060426
835509LV00015B/1573